№ 2300740

BOOK DUE

APR 5 1969

DO NOT REMOVE CARD FROM POCKET

THIS CARD WILL BE PROCESSED BY COMPUTER

(Charge will be made for loss of this card)

D1511807

How to Draw SHAKESPEARE'S PEOPLE

by Arthur Zaidenberg

Abelard-Schuman
London New York Toronto

BOOKS BY ARTHUR ZAIDENBERG

How to Draw Athletes in Action
How to Draw Birds, Fish and Reptiles
How to Draw Butterflies, Bees and Beetles
How to Draw Costumes and Clothes
How to Draw Dogs, Cats and Horses
How to Draw Farm Animals
How to Draw Flowers, Fruit and Vegetables
How to Draw Heads and Faces
How to Draw Historic and Modern Bridges
How to Draw Landscapes, Seascapes and Cityscapes
How to Draw Military and Civilian Uniforms
How to Draw Period Costumes
How to Draw Shakespeare's People
How to Draw Ships and Trains, Cars and Airplanes
How to Draw Wild Animals

© Copyright 1967 by Arthur Zaidenberg
Library of Congress Catalogue Card Number: 67-18121

London	*New York*	*Toronto*
Abelard-Schuman	Abelard-Schuman	Abelard-Schuman
Limited	Limited	Canada Limited
8 King St. WC2	6 West 57th St.	896 Queen St. W.

Printed in the United States of America

Contents

Introduction

Each of us conjures up a different image of the characters we read about in novels and in plays. We come to know them through the author's description, as well as through their words and actions; but it is our own imagination which must create visual pictures of them.

Shakespeare's dramatic powers and rich use of language bring his characters vividly to life. Still, it is left to our own fantasy to interpret their appearance. At one time or another, everyone has had the experience of imagining how some fictional hero or villain looks, only to have that image shattered by an entirely different interpretation of a book illustrator, or an actor cast in that role in a film or on the stage.

It is hoped that HOW TO DRAW SHAKESPEARE'S PEOPLE may serve as a stimulant to your imagination, and an aid in drawing the fascinating characters as you "see" them in your mind's eye.

The short resumés of the plays which are dealt with in this book make no attempt to be all-inclusive; they are provided only as a guide to the nature of the scenes in which the characters exist. It is hoped that these pages will stimulate also the student's interest in reading—and seeing in the theater—many of the tragedies and comedies of Shakespeare.

The versions of the main characters in the selected plays were chosen only as examples of the factors required in the process of conceiving and drawing your own interpretation of the exciting people of Shakespeare's plays.

The "scaffold" figures demonstrate that it is not necessary to make detailed, "realistic" drawings of these men and women. Try to draw their nobility or villainy, their rage or their violence, in very easy terms. Set the "stage" in your mind and draw the cast of characters with great simplicity, but with all the excitement which they evoke in you as you read about them.

Basic Drawing Materials

The drawings in this book were made with the familiar writing tools we all learned to use at school, pencil and pen and ink.

For warmth and variety in the quality of the line and tone of shading, the pencils were carbon instead of lead. They may be bought at any art supply shop. Get a range of three labeled HB, B and BB.

You will need a sandblock for pointing your pencils, and also a soap eraser—but use it sparingly.

Get a pocket sketch pad and acquire the habit of making quick, simple sketches of people about you.

For your pen and ink drawings, use crow quill pens and India ink. Its deep black quality is best for drawing.

There are a great many other drawing materials, but those listed above will give you a wide range and much pleasure if used freely and thoughtfully.

The Human Body

The human body is a very complex machine. To learn about all the innumerable muscles and bones of the body would take much time and study and many more pages than we have available here.

Fortunately, for our purposes all that needs to be aimed at is the ability to draw a reasonably proportionate simplification of the human figure.

Once you begin to see the body in these simple forms, it becomes relatively easy to draw it in various actions and positions that will portray the actors in our plays in a basic way.

Bear in mind that you are not a camera. It is not the function of even a professional artist to reproduce everything he sees exactly.

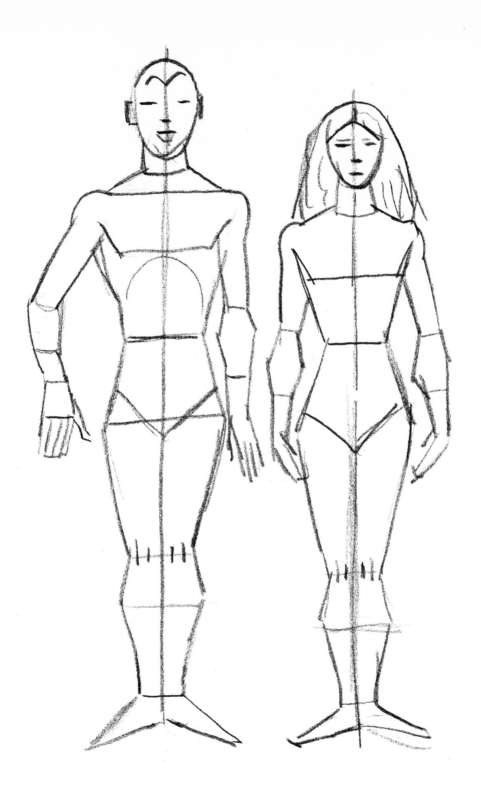

8

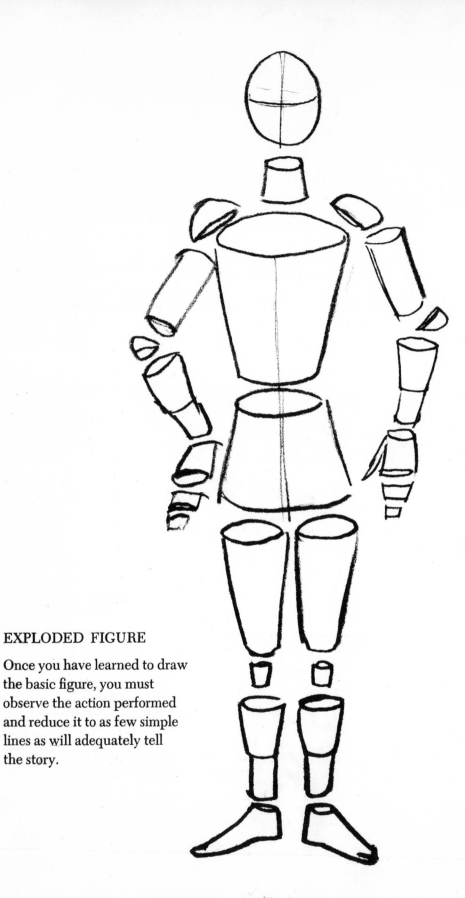

EXPLODED FIGURE

Once you have learned to draw
the basic figure, you must
observe the action performed
and reduce it to as few simple
lines as will adequately tell
the story.

THE HEAD

Draw these heads with the features
placed in their proper relation
to each other as the head turns.

EXPRESSION

Experiment with exaggerating
the expressions on the faces
of the characters.

Julius Caesar

This tragedy tells the story of Brutus, a great patriot of Rome, who loves Julius Caesar, his friend, but fears that Caesar's ambition is to become the king of Rome. Brutus enters into a conspiracy with other Roman Senators, among them Cassius, whose motives are less noble. They assassinate Caesar when he appears before the Senate.

Mark Antony speaks to the populace of Rome at Caesar's funeral and rouses them against the assassins. In the ensuing war between the conspirators' army and Mark Antony's followers, the assassins are defeated. Both the noble Brutus and Cassius commit suicide on the battlefield.

After looking over the simple drawings of the figures and of the characters, wearing clothes typical of their era, try to draw your own concept of them.

Characters in the drawings:
Julius Caesar
Calpurnia, Caesar's wife
Brutus, Cassius and Casca, conspirators against Caesar
Mark Antony

JULIUS CAESAR

CALPURNIA
CAESAR'S WIFE

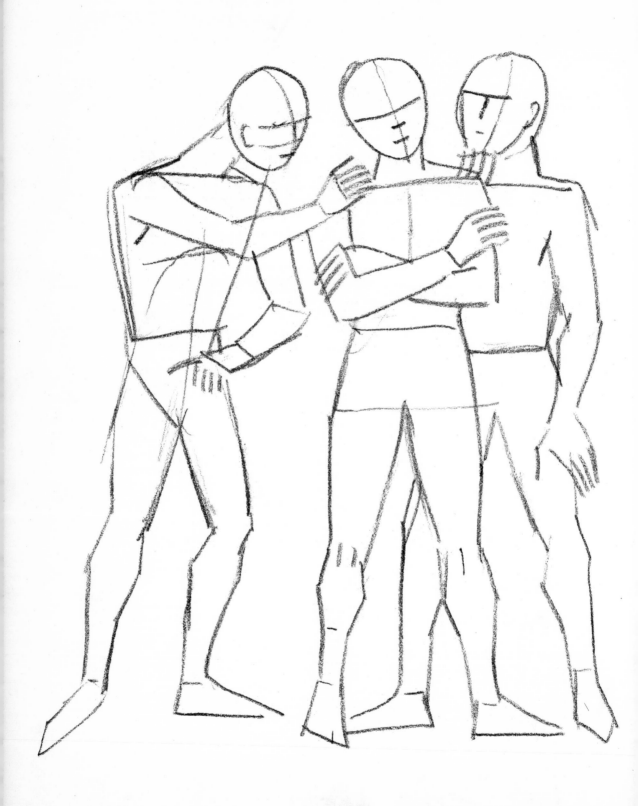

CONSPIRATORS AGAINST JULIUS CAESAR

CASSIUS

BRUTUS

CASCA

ASSASSINATION OF CAESAR

MARK ANTONY

Romeo and Juliet

In the city of Verona, a deadly feud between two families, the Montagues and the Capulets, has caused much bloodshed in the streets. The ruling Prince of Verona declares that anyone violating the peace in the city will suffer severe penalties.

Romeo, Montague's son, goes in disguise to a ball at the palace of the Capulets. There he sees and falls in love with Juliet, Capulet's beautiful daughter. And she falls in love with him.

That night, Romeo climbs the garden walls of the Capulet palace and woos Juliet on her balcony. The next morning, they secretly marry in the cell of Friar Laurence, Romeo's friend.

Later that day, Romeo is in the street with his companion Mercutio. They meet and quarrel with Tybalt, Juliet's cousin. Tybalt challenges and kills Mercutio. Romeo kills Tybalt, and is banished from the city.

Juliet's father orders her to marry a kinsman of the Prince, the Count Paris. Friar Laurence gives Juliet a potion which puts her into a sleep resembling death. Her grief-stricken family places her in the burial vault of the Capulets.

Meanwhile, Friar Laurence has sent a message to Romeo explaining his plot to bring the couple together. Romeo does not receive this message, but his servant arrives with news of Juliet's death.

Romeo resolves to kill himself at the tomb of his beloved. There, at her supposed grave, he drinks poison. When Juliet awakens from her drugged sleep and finds her lover dead, she stabs herself with his dagger and dies.

The two noble families, shattered by grief, join hands and vow eternal peace.

Characters in the drawings:
Montague and Lady Montague
Romeo
Capulet and Lady Capulet
Juliet
Mercutio and Benvolio, Romeo's friends
Tybalt, Juliet's cousin
Juliet's nurse
Paris, kinsman of the Prince of Verona

FRIENDS OF ROMEO
BENVOLIO
MERCUTIO

ROMEO'S FATHER AND MOTHER
MONTAGUE AND
LADY MONTAGUE

JULIET'S FATHER AND MOTHER
CAPULET

LADY CAPULET

PLAN SKETCH

JULIET'S NURSE

TYBALT, COUSIN OF JULIET

PARIS, KINSMAN OF
THE PRINCE OF
VERONA

JULIET

ROMEO

ROMEO AND JULIET (ACT III SCENE I)
Mercutio: "I am hurt.
A plague o' both your houses!"

ROMEO AND JULIET (ACT V SCENE III)
Romeo: "... here, here will I remain
With worms that are thy chamber-maids...."

Othello

Othello, a Moor, has been raised to the rank of general for his brave service to Venice in its war against the Turkish Empire. While he is a visitor at the palace of his friend, Senator Brabantio, he falls in love with Brabantio's daughter, Desdemona. She, in turn, falls in love with the brave general and they are secretly married.

Iago, aide to Othello—resentful of being secondary in rank to Cassio, another aide—hates the general.

He informs Brabantio of the secret marriage, and the angry father denounces Othello as a black sorcerer who used witchcraft to win his daughter. The Duke of Venice absolves Othello and appoints him to lead the forces of Venice against the Turks.

Iago conspires against Cassio and succeeds by crafty deceit in turning Othello against him.

By subtle plotting, he also tricks Othello into thinking that Desdemona is unfaithful. Iago obtains a treasured handkerchief which Othello has given to Desdemona. He places it in Cassio's room and convinces Othello that she gave it to Cassio.

In a fury of jealousy, Othello plots with Iago to kill Cassio in a street brawl, but Cassio is only wounded. Then, Othello smothers his beloved Desdemona.

Too late, proof of Desdemona's innocence and Iago's villainy are brought to Othello. He wounds Iago and kills himself. Iago is executed by the State of Venice.

Characters in the drawings:
Othello, the Moor of Venice
Cassio, a lieutenant
Bianca
Desdemona, Othello's wife
Senator Brabantio
Iago
Emilia, Iago's wife

OTHELLO
THE MOOR OF VENICE

CASSIO

BIANCA

DESDEMONA
WIFE OF OTHELLO

SENATOR BRABANTIO

EMILIA
WIFE OF IAGO

OTHELLO (ACT III SCENE III)
Iago: "I will in Cassio's lodging lose this napkin,
And let him find it. Trifles light as air
Are to the jealous confirmations strong
As proofs of holy writ. . . ."

Hamlet

Hamlet encounters the ghost of his dead father. The ghost reveals that he was murdered by his own brother Claudius, who is now King of Denmark and married to the widowed Queen, Hamlet's mother.

Hamlet is distraught. He decides to expose the King, his uncle. He hires a company of strolling players to enact the story of the murder before the King, the Queen and their court. At the critical moment, the King rises and rushes away, betraying his guilt. Hamlet resolves to kill him.

When Hamlet accuses the Queen of conspiracy with the King against his late father, she is filled with remorse.

Polonius, adviser to the royal pair—who is the father of Ophelia, Hamlet's beloved, and of Laertes, Hamlet's best friend—is spying behind the curtain. Hamlet mistakes him for the King and stabs him with his sword.

Ophelia goes mad with grief and is drowned. At her funeral, the King incites Laertes to revenge, urging him to engage Hamlet in a fencing match. The foil given to Laertes is poisoned, and the King also prepares a poisoned drink for Hamlet, should he escape the foil.

Unknowingly, the Queen toasts Hamlet with the poisoned drink. Fencing, Laertes wounds Hamlet and is himself wounded by the same sword. Hamlet turns on the King, stabs him—and then dies.

Characters in the drawings:
Hamlet
Queen Gertrude, Hamlet's mother
Claudius, King of Denmark, Hamlet's uncle
Polonius
Ophelia, daughter of Polonius
Laertes, son of Polonius

HAMLET (ACT II SCENE II)

Hamlet: "... the play's the thing
Wherein I'll catch the conscience of the King."

PRINCE HAMLET

QUEEN GERTRUDE
HAMLET'S
MOTHER

CLAUDIUS, HAMLET'S UNCLE
KING OF DENMARK

LAERTES
BROTHER OF OPHELIA
SON OF POLONIUS

POLONIUS

OPHELIA

HAMLET (ACT V SCENE I)
Hamlet: "Alas, poor Yorick!"

HAMLET (ACT IV SCENE VII)

Queen: "Her clothes spread wide,
    And, mermaid-like, awhile they bore her up. . . ."

Antony and Cleopatra

Mark Antony, a great leader of Rome and a conquering general, becomes infatuated with Cleopatra, the beautiful young queen of Egypt. He neglects his duties to Rome and lingers in Egypt beside her.

Hearing of an attack upon the city by Pompey, a rival for power, Antony is called back to Rome. There he marries Octavia, the sister of Octavius Caesar, another powerful Roman leader.

But Antony cannot stay away from Cleopatra, and he leaves his bride to return to Egypt. Caesar uses the desertion of his sister as an excuse to break Antony's power in Rome. He sends a fleet to attack the combined fleets of Antony and Egypt.

Antony is defeated in a fierce land battle. A false report of Cleopatra's death overcomes him with grief and he stabs himself. He dies after a last meeting with her.

Cleopatra, in despair and fearing to be brought to Rome in chains, allows a poisonous asp to sting her and she, too, dies.

Characters in the drawings:
Cleopatra
Charmian, Cleopatra's servant
Mark Antony
Octavius Caesar
Octavia, Antony's wife

CHARMIAN

CLEOPATRA

OCTAVIA,
WIFE OF ANTONY

OCTAVIUS
CAESAR

MARK
ANTONY

Macbeth

Three weird witches intercept Macbeth and Banquo, two Scottish generals returning from a victorious battle against the Thane of Cawdor, who attacked their king, Duncan. The witches prophesy that Macbeth will become king and that Banquo will be the father of kings.

The ambitious Macbeth returns to his castle. There, his equally ambitious wife plots with him to kill King Duncan, who is visiting them.

They drug the guards and Macbeth murders the sleeping king. Lady Macbeth smears blood on the guards so that they will appear guilty, and Macbeth, simulating grief, kills them.

Now king of Scotland, Macbeth fears the suspicion of Banquo and the prophecy of the witches that Banquo's heirs would be Scotland's kings. He arranges to have Banquo murdered also.

Haunted by the ghosts of his victims, Macbeth seeks out the witches and demands to know more of the future. They tell him that he will remain king until the forest near his castle, Birnam Wood, moves to overthrow him. Reassured by this prophecy, he returns to find that Lady Macbeth has gone mad with remorse and fear.

Malcolm, son of Duncan, raises an army against Macbeth. Approaching the castle, he orders each of his men to cut a limb from the trees of Birnam Wood to camouflage their attack.

Horrified and desperate, Macbeth attempts to make a last stand and is slain by Macduff, a loyal general of the late King Duncan.

Characters in the drawings:
Macbeth
The Three Witches
Lady Macbeth
Doctor
Lady in waiting

MACBETH AND THE THREE WITCHES

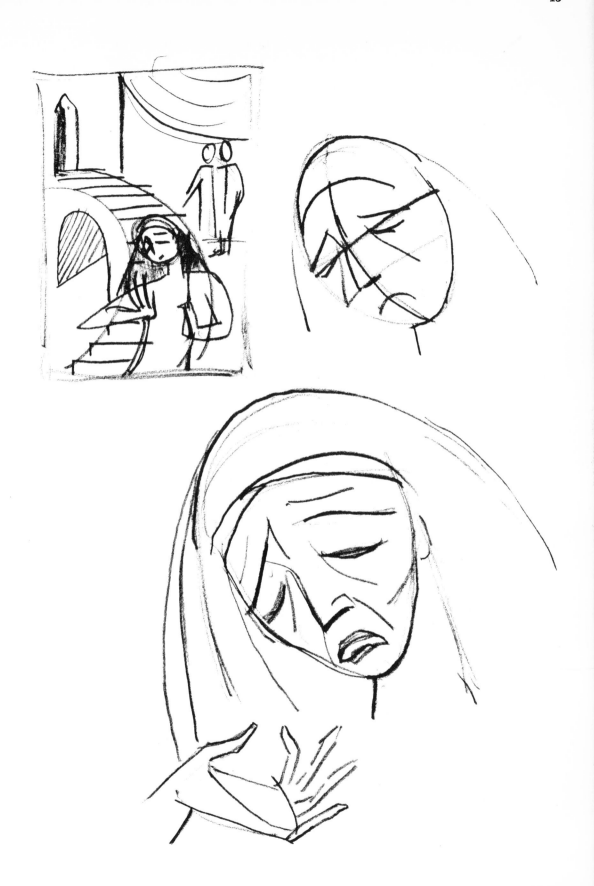

50

DOCTOR

LADY
IN
WAITING

LADY MACBETH

King Lear

King Lear of ancient Britain, in his old age, divides his kingdom between Regan and Goneril, his two fawning and flattering daughters. He gives nothing to his honest daughter Cordelia, who really loves him but will not flatter him.

Cordelia marries the King of France and leaves England.

Lear is cruelly abused by his other two daughters now that they have the kingdom in their hands. Eventually he is turned out of his castle in the midst of a raging storm, accompanied only by his two faithful friends, the Earl of Kent and a jester, the King's Fool. The harsh and ungrateful acts of Goneril and Regan have driven the old king mad.

The Earl of Gloucester, who is loyal to Lear, is also betrayed— by one of his own sons, the ruthlessly ambitious Edmund. Blinded by the conspirators, Gloucester is cared for by his devoted son Edgar.

Cordelia arrives with an army from France to aid her father, but the French are defeated and she and King Lear are taken captive. Cordelia is put to death and the old king dies of grief.

The evil Goneril poisons Regan and then kills herself.

Characters in the drawings:
King Lear
Fool
Goneril, Regan and Cordelia, King Lear's daughters
King of France, Cordelia's husband
Edgar, Gloucester's son
Edmund, Edgar's half brother

KING LEAR (ACT III SCENE II)

Enter Lear and Fool

Lear: "Blow, winds, and crack your cheeks!"

KING OF FRANCE
HUSBAND OF CORDELIA

GONERIL   REGAN   CORDELIA

KING LEAR'S DAUGHTERS

EDGAR, SON OF GLOUCESTER

EDMUND,
HALF BROTHER OF
EDGAR

A Midsummer Night's Dream

The setting of this comedy is a fanciful and fairyland Athens of Shakespeare's imagination.

Lysander and Hermia are very much in love, but Egeus, Hermia's father, evokes the law of Athens which requires her to marry Demetrius, the man he has chosen for her. Theseus, Duke of Athens, must uphold the law of his realm.

Hermia and Lysander flee to the woods around Athens to escape the order of the law. Hermia's friend, Helena, who is in love with Demetrius, tells him where Hermia and Lysander are hiding out. Demetrius pursues the lovers, and Helena follows him.

The forest is ruled by the fairy king and queen, Oberon and Titania. Oberon instructs Puck, a hobgoblin, to put a potion in the eyes of Demetrius which will cause him to fall in love with Helena. Puck mistakes Lysander for Demetrius and pours the potion in *his* eyes.

Lysander awakes and, seeing Helena, falls in love with her and follows her into the deep woods. There is much quarreling among the four lovers before Puck sets matters straight by removing the spell of the potion.

Meanwhile, some Athenians, meeting in the woods, are the butt of the playful Puck, who puts an ass's head on a simple Athenian craftsman, Bottom. The fairy queen Titania, having been given the love potion, falls in love with Bottom and commands the fairies to wait on him and adorn him.

After many amusing confusions, the spell of the potion wears off and the wedding of the Duke of Athens and Hippolyta is celebrated.

Characters in the drawings:
Titania, fairy queen
Bottom
Oberon, fairy king
Puck
Theseus, Duke of Athens
Lysander
Demetrius

A MIDSUMMER NIGHT'S DREAM (ACT IV SCENE I)

Titania: "And kiss thy fair large ears, my gentle joy."

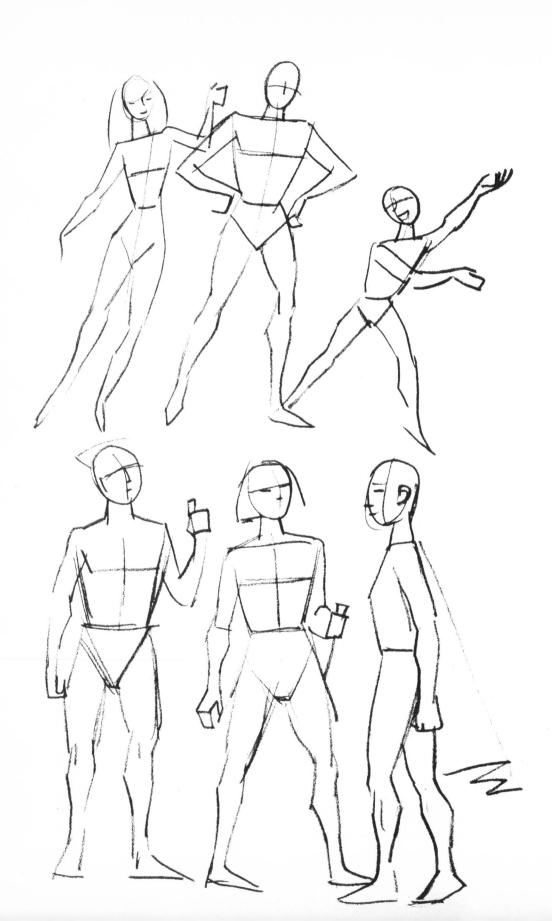

TITANIA, FAIRY QUEEN

OBERON, KING OF FAIRIES

PUCK

DEMETRIUS WHO LOVES HERMIA

LYSANDER WHO LOVES HERMIA

THESEUS, DUKE OF ATHENS

The Taming of the Shrew

To Padua comes a student, Lucentio. He hears a rich merchant announce that his gentle daughter Bianca cannot marry either of her two suitors until someone is found to marry his violent-tempered daughter Katharina.

Lucentio disguises himself as a teacher and obtains the position of tutor to Bianca, with whom he has fallen in love.

A gay and carefree young man, Petruchio, arrives in Padua in search of a rich wife. Bianca's suitors persuade him to ask for the hand of Katharina. Her father is delighted, and Petruchio announces to the assembled guests that he will return in a few days to marry Katharina. She is furious, but baffled by his continued praises no matter how badly she raves and insults him.

When Petruchio returns, he is mounted on a decrepit horse and is followed by a servant who, like Petruchio, is outlandishly dressed. Petruchio behaves in a wild, crazy manner during the ceremony and carries off Katharina, screaming that he will save her from the thieves and murderers who would harm her.

After a dismal journey on his miserable horse, they arrive at his home, where the servants have been instructed to participate in the plot to "tame the shrew." Under the pretext that nothing is good enough for his bride, Petruchio smashes the dishes served to her and tears her bed apart. Then, sleepless and hungry, Katharina is forced to go through a stormy session with a tailor whom Petruchio reviles for his incompetence.

When the time comes to go to her sister's wedding, she has no new clothes. She is weak and has lost all resistance to the unpredictable, violent ways of Petruchio.

At the feast given by the merchant to celebrate the marriage of his two daughters, Katharina amazes the guests with her meek devotion to Petruchio. She advises the young women to be obedient and loving to their husbands.

The shrew has been tamed.

Characters in the drawings:
Katharina
Petruchio
Baptista, Katharina's father
Hortensio and Lucentio, Bianca's suitors

Katharina: "I chafe you, if I tarry: let me go."

62

BAPTISTA,
FATHER OF KATHARINA

BIANCA'S SUITORS
HORTENSIO   LUCENTIO

PETRUCHIO AND KATHARINA

Final Word

In these pages you have only *begun* two projects which can enrich your whole life: learning to draw, and the understanding of some of Shakespeare's people. The two projects combined will help each other.

The colorful people of Shakespeare will assume physical appearance from your attempts to picture them, and your drawings will gain stature from the noble lines which describe the people you draw.

Your drawings should be extremely simple. You may only capture one action or one mood of each complex character, but in trying to draw them you will, in a way, create your own Shakespeare theatre. You will be casting the play, directing the scene, choosing the costumes, and, in the process, learning to draw.